✠

St Albans

Other titles available in this series

ST ALBANS

*Diane
With love
Bill Ritson*

Bill Ritson

Illustrated by
David Pepin

*From the author to me
and
From me to you.
With love on your
birthday.
Always,
Diane*

CANTERBURY
PRESS
Norwich

Text © Bill Ritson 1998
Illustrations © David Pepin 1998

First published in 1998 by The Canterbury Press Norwich
(a publishing imprint of Hymns Ancient & Modern Limited
a registered charity)
St Mary's Works, St Mary's Plain
Norwich, Norfolk NR3 3BH

British Library Cataloguing in Publication Data

A catalogue record for this book is available
from the British Library

ISBN 1-85311-210-0

Typeset by Rowland Phototypesetting Ltd,
Bury St Edmunds, Suffolk IP32 6NU
Printed and bound in Great Britain by
Redwood Books, Trowbridge, Wilts

Contents

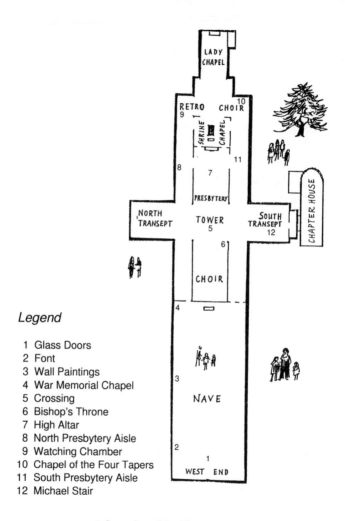

Legend

1 Glass Doors
2 Font
3 Wall Paintings
4 War Memorial Chapel
5 Crossing
6 Bishop's Throne
7 High Altar
8 North Presbytery Aisle
9 Watching Chamber
10 Chapel of the Four Tapers
11 South Presbytery Aisle
12 Michael Stair

A floor plan of St Albans Cathedral

Introduction

Welcome to the Cathedral and Abbey Church of St Alban. This building is usually known as St Albans Abbey, or to local people simply as the Abbey, because until 1539 it was the Abbey Church of the medieval monastery. In 1539 it became, and still is, a parish church. In 1877, when the Diocese of St Albans was founded, it also became a Cathedral.

Pilgrims have been coming to this site for more than 1,700 years, because it was here, in the middle of the third century, that St Alban was martyred – nearly 400 years before St Augustine landed at Canterbury in 597.

St Albans Cathedral seen from the south

The Glass Doors

Outside the West End of the building in medieval times there would have been throngs of people and the sound of the pilgrim market, with all its hustle and bustle of buying and selling. As we enter through the West End we are faced by two glass doors. The right-hand door welcomes us with the words, 'Seek Him that made the seven stars and Orion' – a quotation from the Old Testament prophet Amos:

> Seek him that made the seven stars and Orion and turns the shadow of death into the morning and makes the day dark with night; that calls for the waters of the sea and pours them out upon the face of the earth: the Lord is his Name (Amos 5:8).

These words encourage us, as we enter the building, to seek God, to look for the Lord.

The left-hand door welcomes us with some words taken from the Apocrypha: 'I will light a candle of understanding in thine heart' 2 Esdras 14:25 – words expressing the hope that we may find light and understanding in this place, that it may help us to glimpse a little of the glory and wonder of God.

Engraved in the glass above the doors is the figure of the young Jesus standing in front of his mother. He is holding up his arms in welcome, but he is also reminding us of his arms opened wide on the Cross. To one side of him is a unicorn (a symbol of purity) and on the other side is a peacock (a symbol of resurrection).

The West End

Prayer

As we enter the Cathedral, let us pray in the words of this ancient Celtic prayer:

I weave a silence on to my lips.
I weave a silence into my mind.
I weave a silence within my heart.

Calm me, O Lord, as you stilled the storm.
Still me, O Lord, keep me from harm.
Let all the tumult within me cease.
Enfold me, Lord, in your peace.

✠

O Lord, send out Thy light and Thy truth,
that they may lead me;
and bring me unto Thy holy hill
and to Thy dwelling.

*

God said to Moses of the burning bush,
'Take off your shoes,
for the place where you stand is holy ground.'

*

Jacob said, 'Surely the Lord is in this place;
this is none other but the house of God;
this is the gate of Heaven.' Amen.

St Alban

At the time when St Alban lived, the ground on which the Cathedral now stands was just a grassy hill outside the Roman city of Verulamium. Remains of the city can still be found at the bottom of the hill.

Alban, a citizen of Verulamium, who some say was a soldier, gave shelter to a Christian priest who was fleeing from his pursuers in a time of persecution. He was converted by the priest to the Christian faith. Some days later, the pursuers came to his house searching for the priest. Alban, wearing the priest's long cloak, allowed the other man time to escape. He then opened the door and gave himself up in the priest's place.

He was bound and led before a judge. When he was asked his name he declared, 'My name is Alban and I worship and adore the true and living God.' He refused to renounce Christ or worship the Emperor, and so was condemned to death. He was led up the hill to be beheaded. It is said that as his head fell, his executioner's eyes dropped out on to the ground. According to the Venerable Bede (the eighth-century author of *A History of the English Church and People*), Alban was martyred in about the year 250. He was the first Christian martyr in Britain.

Very soon after Alban was killed, the site of his death began to be revered as a holy place. A shrine was built, and by the end of the fourth century there was a church. Saint Germanus, Bishop of Auxerre, came here in the year 429 and was most impressed by the faith of the local Christian community.

Prayer

On the inside of the glass doors is engraved the Alban Prayer:

Almighty God,
we thank you for this place,
built to your glory
and in memory of Alban,
our first Martyr.
Following his example, in the fellowship of
the saints,
may we worship and adore the true and living God
and be faithful witnesses to the Christ
who is alive and reigns now and for ever. Amen.

The Nave

As we look up the Nave we cannot help noticing the different styles of architecture. We know that there was a church on this site by the year 429 and that in 793 King Offa founded a Benedictine monastery here. When the Normans arrived in the eleventh century they pulled down the earlier Saxon building and built a church of their own, using bricks and other materials from the old Roman city of Verulamium. These bricks were already 600 years old in 1077.

The rounded arches at the front of the north (left) side of the Nave, the Tower and the Transept walls (to which we shall come later) were built in the time of the first Norman Abbot, Paul de Caen. Paul was the nephew of Lanfranc, the Archbishop of Canterbury.

Later, in the twelfth century, Abbot John de Cella enlarged the building, adding the five bays with pointed arches at the back on the north (left) and the four at the back on the south (right). These were built in the Early English style, using Totternhoe clunch, quarried near Dunstable.

The five bays at the front on the south (right) are more decorated than those at the rear, and they replaced columns which had collapsed in 1323.

No one was killed, although it was later believed that two monks and a boy had died. High up above the choir stalls on this south side we can see effigies of the heads of King Edward II and his wife Queen Isabella, and also Abbot Hugh of Eversden and the master mason Henry Wy, who were responsible for rebuilding the arches.

The more pointed arches can perhaps remind us that our hearts and minds need to be pointed heavenwards. The earlier, more rounded arches, which begin to go up and then come back down, can remind us that although our lives may be heaven-ward bound, they are lived here on earth. As our Lord Jesus Christ said, 'Thy will be done on earth as it is in heaven.'

The Nave

Prayer

God be in my head
And in my understanding.
God be in mine eyes
And in my looking.
God be in my mouth
And in my speaking.
God be in my heart
And in my thinking.
God be at mine end
And at my departing.

Sarum Primer

The Font

Near the back of the Nave on the north (left) is the
Font, where new members are welcomed into the
Church (the Christian family) by baptism with water.
Near the Font is a picture of the monastery at
St Albans before it was dissolved by Henry VIII.
Now only the Abbey Church and the Abbey Gate-
house survive.

Prayer

Almighty God, keep us faithful to our baptism and so make us ready for that day when the whole creation shall be made perfect in your Son, our Saviour Jesus Christ.

The Font

The Wall Paintings

In medieval times, the Nave would have been a blaze of colour. The thirteenth-century west-facing wall paintings on the oldest pillars show crucifixion scenes and, below these, scenes from the life of the Blessed Virgin Mary. Facing inwards are bigger pictures of (from west to east) St Christopher, St Thomas of Canterbury, St Zita of Lucca, and St Alban with St Amphibalus. St Christopher, the patron saint of travellers, is pictured carrying the Christ child on his shoulder across a river.

St Thomas of Canterbury (Thomas Becket) was martyred in his cathedral on 29 December 1170. When he became Archbishop of Canterbury Thomas, as he himself put it, changed from being 'a patron of play-actors and a follower of hounds to being a shepherd of souls.' He was killed for trying to defend the Church against the royal power of King Henry II. His last words were 'Willingly I die for the name of Jesus and in defence of the Church.' In his play *Murder in the Cathedral*, which is about the killing of St Thomas, T. S. Eliot wrote:

> For wherever a saint has dwelt, wherever a martyr
>   has given his blood for Christ,
> There is holy ground and the sanctity shall not
>   depart from it,
> Though armies trample over it, though sightseers
>   come with guidebooks looking over it;

From such ground springs that which forever
renews the earth.

St Zita of Lucca in Italy is the patron saint of all those
who work in the kitchen. Here she is depicted as
wearing a long dress, and it looks as if she is standing on a table. It is lovely that an Italian kitchen-maid
should have been chosen to adorn the side of a pillar
in an English monastery.

St Alban and St Amphibalus are pictured together.
Amphibalus was the name or nickname of the priest
who sought refuge in Alban's house and converted
him to Christianity. The name comes from the Greek
word for 'cloak' and so is a reference to the cloak-
swapping in Alban's story. The Venerable Bede says
of Amphibalus, 'Christ's confessor, whose time of
martyrdom had not yet come, lay hidden in Alban's
house.' This suggests that Amphibalus too later suf-
fered as a martyr.

The Nave was traditionally the part of the Abbey
Church where the people were allowed to gather.
The part behind the screen was reserved for the
monks. The monks would come into the nave on
great festivals. Also, those monks who were priests
would say mass at altars at the feet of some of the
pillars (below the Crucifixion paintings). Medieval
pilgrims might have gathered here to confess their
sins before going on up to the Shrine.

Today the Nave is where a huge congregation
gathers for the Parish Eucharist every Sunday

morning. It is also used for other Sunday services, for diocesan services such as ordinations and confirmations, for ecumenical, civic and youth services, for school services, for concerts and lectures, for university award ceremonies, for exhibitions, for harvest suppers and for parish parties. It is still very much a place for the people.

The Choir in the Nave

Prayers

> Praise to the Lord, the Almighty, the King
> of Creation;
> O my soul, praise Him, for He is thy health
> and salvation.
> Come ye who hear,
> Brothers and sisters draw near,
> Praise Him in glad adoration.

English Hymnal, 536

> O all ye works of the Lord, bless ye the Lord:
> Praise Him and magnify Him for ever.

Book of Common Prayer

O Thou who hast made us for Thyself, make our restless hearts to find their rest in Thee.

St Augustine (adapted)

The Pulpit, the Lectern and the Altar

At the front of the Nave are the pulpit, where the sermon is preached at services, and the lectern, where the Bible is read. The eagle on the lectern symbolizes the Gospel of Christ being carried to the whole world.

The screen behind the Altar was constructed by Abbot Thomas de la Mare in about 1350. The cross is sixteenth-century Spanish crystal and was presented to the Abbey in the 1920s.

At the Altar bread is taken, blessed, broken and given, and wine is taken, blessed and given. As we do this, so we remember and celebrate the presence with us of Jesus, our Risen and Living Lord, who gave himself – his body and his blood – on the Cross. In the Holy Communion, he comes to be with us, to feed us, to give us his life. For our part, we offer him our lives.

The lectern

Love bade me welcome; yet my soul drew back,
Guilty of dust and sin.
But quick-eyed Love, observing me grow slack
From my first entrance in,
Drew nearer to me, sweetly questioning,
If I lacked anything.
'A guest,' I answered, 'worthy to be here.'
Love said, 'You shall be he.'
'I the unkind, ungrateful? Ah, my dear,
I cannot look on thee.'
Love took my hand, and smiling did reply,
'Who made the eyes but I?'
'Truth, Lord, but I have marred them; let my shame
Go where it doth deserve.'
'And you know not,' says Love, 'who bore the
blame?'
'My dear, then I will serve.'
'You must sit down,' says Love, 'and taste my meat.'
So I did sit and eat.

George Herbert (1593–1633)

Behold the Lamb of God who takes away the sins of the world.
Happy are those who are called to his supper.

*

Lord, I am not worthy to receive you,
but say the word only and I shall be healed.

*

The War Memorial Chapel

To the left of the Altar, at the top of the north aisle, is a War Memorial Chapel commemorating those who died in wars so that we may live in peace. And, looking back down the Nave, we can see the West Window, which is filled with stained glass designed in 1925 by Sir Ninian Comper as a war memorial.

Prayer

O God, whose will is to fold both heaven and earth in a single peace; let the design of your great love lighten upon the waste of our angers and sorrows; and give peace to your Church, peace among nations, peace in our homes, and peace in our hearts; through your Son, our Saviour, Jesus Christ.

The organ, rebuilt by Harrison and Harrison of Durham in 1962, is one of the finest cathedral organs in the country. An International Organ Festival is held at St Albans every other year.

If we then go through the glass screen doors, on the wall on the right we will see a notice about the Tomb of the Hermits, named after Roger of Markyate and Sigar of Northaw. Roger was the mentor of St Christina of Markyate. Sigar walked every night to the service at the Abbey. It is said that he chased away and banished the nightingales from Northaw Wood, as they disturbed his meditation. It is also said that because of this, to this day, the nightingales have never returned.

Moving on, in the South Transept at the entrance to the Crossing is a prayer-board on which visitors may leave their petitions, intercessions, thanksgivings and other requests for prayer. There is also an opportunity to light a candle. Some of the prayers on the board are used as part of the intercessions at Evensong on weekday evenings. Every morning and evening we also pray in turn for churches dedicated to St Alban all over the world, from Arcata in California to Wagga Wagga in Australia.

The Crossing

The ceiling here is 102 feet above ground level. The painted coats of arms are replicas (made in 1951) of the fifteenth-century originals. The red and white roses of York and Lancaster can be seen, reminding us of the Battles of St Albans during the Wars of the Roses (1455–85). The first of these battles was fought in St Albans in 1455, when the Yorkists won. The second Battle of St Albans was won by the Lancastrians in 1461. The Lancastrian troops did not behave well, and sacked the Abbey.

The tower above is built of Roman brick from the old city of Verulamium. We can see the round Norman arches. In the tower there is a peal of twelve bells.

The tower

The Quire

The Quire is the part of the Abbey where the monks said their prayers (called the Daily Offices) seven times a day, following the Rule of St Benedict. It reminds us that the whole building is primarily a place of prayer.

The present choir-stalls are Victorian, and it is here that the Cathedral clergy still gather together before breakfast every weekday morning to say Matins or Morning Prayer. This is followed by a celebration of Holy Communion at a different altar each day.

On weekday afternoons they gather together again for Evensong or Evening Prayer, which is sung by the boy or girl choristers. There is no choir school, and the choristers attend different schools in the city. They practise before school in the morning and again after school in the afternoon. On Saturdays the Choirmen or Lay Clerks join the boys (or girls) to sing Evensong here in the Quire. Some of the Sunday services are held here, while others are held in the Nave. The Cathedral choir sings at two or three services on Sundays.

The clergy are led by the Dean. The other clergy at the Cathedral are known as Canons. The Dean and Canons sit in the seats or 'stalls' at the far end of the Quire, facing the Altar.

The stalls in the back row on either side are the seats belonging to twenty-two Honorary Canons who do not work at the Cathedral, but are parish priests in the Diocese who have been given the title 'Canon'. The Honorary Canon can sit in his or her stall whenever he or she comes to the Cathedral for a service in the Quire. It is pleasing to imagine that Canon Frederick Chasuble – the Rector of Woolton in Hertfordshire in Oscar Wilde's play *The Importance of Being Ernest* – was an Honorary Canon of St Albans.

From the pulpit here, during the summer, prayers are said on the hour every hour throughout the day to remind visitors, and everyone in the building, that this is first and foremost a House of God. Everyone keeps silence for a moment.

The Bishop's throne is known as the Cathedra. It is here that the Bishop sits when he comes to services in this part of the building. He looks after the whole Diocese of St Albans (which includes Hertfordshire, Bedfordshire, Luton and part of the London Borough of Barnet), and so he is usually in one of the parishes rather than at his Cathedral, the mother church. Among the Bishops of St Albans has been Robert Runcie, who moved on from here to become Archbishop of Canterbury.

The ceiling in the Quire consists of sixty-six painted panels. Every other panel bears the monogram 'IHS' – the first three letters of the name 'Jesus' in Greek, or the initial letters of the Latin words for 'Jesus Saviour of Men', or (if it is easier to remember) the initial letters of 'In His Service'. This monogram reminds us, as we look up, that it is Jesus, Our Lord and Saviour, whom we serve.

Prayer

Teach us, good Lord, to serve thee as thou deservest; to give and not to count the cost; to fight and not to heed the wounds; to toil and not to seek for rest; to labour and not to ask for any reward, save that of knowing that we do thy will; through Jesus Christ our Lord.

St Ignatius Loyola

The Presbytery

The High Altar Screen

Up the steps is what we call the Presbytery, and then beyond the altar rails is the High Altar, with the tremendous screen behind it. This was erected in the time of Abbot William of Wallingford in the fifteenth century. There is a similar screen at Winchester Cathedral and a later version at St Louis Cathedral in the United States.

The original figures on the screen were destroyed in the sixteenth and seventeenth centuries, and the present statues, carved by Harry Hems of Exeter, date from Victorian times. St Alban and St Amphibalus are on either side of the Altar, while the Blessed Virgin Mary and St John are on either side of Christ.

In the top right-hand corner is the Venerable Bede, who mentions St Albans in his eighth-century book, *A History of the English Church and People*.

Next to Bede is Pope Adrian IV, the only English pope. His real name was Nicholas Breakspear. When he was a boy he applied to join the monastery here at St Albans, but the Abbot told him that he was not good enough and refused to accept him. So off he went to apply to a monastery at Avignon in France, where he was accepted. And so began an ecclesiastical career which eventually culminated in his election as Pope.

Other saints on the screen include St Augustine, St Benedict, St Cuthbert (with an otter at his feet), St Edmund, St Hugh, St Cecilia, St Etheldreda, St Helen and St Lucy.

Below the screen and behind the Altar is a reredos depicting Christ rising from the tomb. This is the work of Sir Alfred Gilbert, who also designed the statue of Eros in Piccadilly Circus. The reredos includes coloured paua-shells from New Zealand.

The High Altar screen

26

The Monks

The monastery at St Albans was for a long time the senior Benedictine House in England. It had daughter cells at places like Tynemouth in Northumberland and Binham Priory in Norfolk.

While the Chapter House was being built in the late 1970s, the remains of eleven abbots and four other monks were discovered. In 1979 these remains were reburied in the Presbytery under a slab at the top of the steps. On the slab are these words:

> Here rest the mortal remains
> of Abbots from 1077 to 1401:
> Paul of Caen,
> Richard d'Albini,
> Geoffrey of Gorron,
> Ralph Gubion,
> Robert of Gorron,
> Simon Warin of Cambridge,
> John de Cella,
> William of Trumpington,
> John of Hertford,
> John de la Moote,
> And also of
> Robert of the Chamber, father of Pope Adrian IV,
> Adam the Cellarer,
> Prior Adam Wittenham,
> Adam Rous, Surgeon to Edward III.
> Removed in 1978 from the Chapter House.
> 'Seek First
> The Kingdom of God.'

One of the people whose remains lie here is Robert of the Chamber, the father of Pope Adrian IV. Robert was a father and a widower before he became a monk. Another person mentioned on the slab is Adam the Cellarer, whose name has been given to an annual autumn Cellarer's Feast to which the Dean invites all the Honorary Canons with their partners.

The most famous monk at St Albans was the historian Matthew Paris, who entered the monastery in 1217 and died in 1259. His real surname is not known, but he was educated in Paris and so called himself Matthew Paris. He was the Abbey's chronicler and is now admired as the greatest of all thirteenth-century chroniclers. His writing is full of interest, and he himself seems to have been interested in everything in the Abbey, in the country and in the world. He was not afraid to criticize kings or popes.

Matthew was equally skilled at writing and drawing. The Cathedral bookshop sells postcards of some of his drawings, including an elephant in a procession. Matthew drew this before he had ever seen an elephant, so he used pattern books provided from Rome. The pattern-book elephants had no knees, just straight legs. But in 1254 King Louis IX of France sent a real, live elephant to King Henry III. It was kept in the Tower of London for four years, until it died. While it was there Matthew made careful drawings of it and realized that it had knees. Thereafter Matthew drew his elephants accurately!

The Cathedral Education Centre arranges some very popular and successful 'trails' and workshops for children from schools both nearby and far away. For some of these the children dress up as monks in the medieval monastery, playing the roles of Abbot, Cellarer, Guest Master and the rest. Or they might play the part of medieval pilgrims for an hour or so and make the last stage of a perhaps long and dangerous journey to Alban's Shrine, where they will leave gifts and pray.

The head of the Bishop's crozier, carried by the child
who plays the Abbot.

Prayers

Gracious and holy Father, give us wisdom to perceive you, diligence to seek you, patience to wait for you, eyes to behold you, a heart to meditate on you, and a life to proclaim you; through the power of the Spirit of Jesus Christ our Lord.

Saint Benedict

*

Breathe on me, Breath of God,
Fill me with life anew,
That I may love what Thou dost love,
And do what Thou wouldst do.

E. Hatch (1835–89)

The North Transept

This part of the Cathedral is dominated by the glorious Rose Window. Formerly it was made of plain glass arranged in geometrical shapes, but in 1989 the old window was replaced with a wonderful blaze of colour designed by Alan Younger. The changing of the glass was paid for by Laporte Industries of Luton to celebrate their centenary. Beneath the window are some words of St Paul in Latin. The English translation is: 'We have a building from God, a house not made with hands, eternal in the heavens' (2 Corinthians 5:1).

The new window was unveiled on 26 September 1989 by Diana, Princess of Wales, who also planted a tree in the north churchyard on the same day. Princess Diana is remembered for her compassion and care for people in need, especially for those with HIV/AIDS and for those maimed by landmines. And so it is appropriate that the window which she unveiled looks down on the part of the Cathedral in which we particularly remember and pray for persecuted people in all parts of the world today.

The altar here is called the Altar of the Persecuted, and on the board beside it is attached an ever-changing list of places where there is persecution, where people are being imprisoned without trial, tortured and put to death, just as St Alban was martyred all those years ago. In this transept there is also a sculpture by Henry Moore called *Standing Figure*. Perhaps we may see it as a figure standing for truth and peace.

We pray and light candles here for peace and justice in all parts of the world, and especially for those places where people are being persecuted.

The North Transept

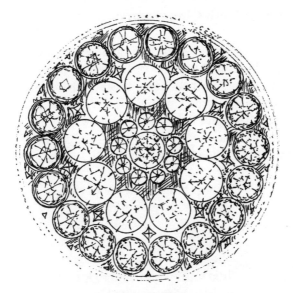

The Rose Window

Prayer

Almighty God, from whom all thoughts of truth
and peace proceed;
kindle, we pray, in the hearts of all
the true love of peace;
and guide with your pure and peaceable wisdom
those who take counsel for the nations of the earth;
that in tranquillity your kingdom may go forward,
till the earth is filled with the knowledge of
your love;
through Jesus Christ our Lord.

Thomas Legh Claughton

The large statue beneath the window is of Thomas Legh Claughton, the first Bishop of St Albans. Earlier in his career he had been Vicar of Kidderminster, where one of his curates was William Walsham How. Walsham How later became a bishop too, but he is best known for his hymns 'For all the Saints' and 'It is a thing most wonderful':

> It is a thing most wonderful,
> Almost too wonderful to be,
> That God's own Son should come from heaven,
> And die to save a child like me.
>
> It is most wonderful to know
> His love for me so free and sure;
> But 'tis more wonderful to see
> My love for Him so faint and poor.
>
> And yet I want to love thee, Lord;
> O light the flame within my heart,
> And I will love thee more and more,
> Until I see thee as thou art.

Lord Grimthorpe

One of the busts here is of Edmund Beckett, Lord Grimthorpe, a very successful nineteenth-century barrister who designed the mechanism for Big Ben, the giant clock in the Houses of Parliament.

The monastery at St Albans was dissolved by King Henry VIII in 1539, and the local townspeople bought the Abbey Church for £400. But it was far too big for them to be able to maintain it over the centuries, and by the late nineteenth century it was in a fairly bad state of repair.

Grimthorpe was the man who came to the rescue. A millionaire and a very strong character, he offered to pay for all the much-needed repairs on condition that he could do exactly as he wanted. He repaired the roof of the Nave and completely rebuilt the West Front to his own design. He also restored the North Transept and the one opposite and the Lady Chapel at the far end. Not everyone approved of his work, but without him St Albans Abbey might by now have looked like Tintern or Fountains or Rievaulx.

St Thomas

The fifteenth-century wall painting to the right of the altar is of St Thomas the Doubter. It was placed here for pilgrims who entered the Abbey by the door in this North Transept on their way to the Shrine. St Thomas can remind us that we all have doubts and find it difficult to believe at times.

Lord, I believe; help thou my unbelief.

*

O Lord God, in whom we live and move and have our being, open our eyes that we may behold thy fatherly presence about us. Draw our hearts to thee by the power of thy love. Teach us to be anxious for nothing, and when we have done what thou hast given us to do, help us, O God our Saviour, to leave the issue to thy wisdom. Take from us all doubt and mistrust. Lift our thoughts up to thee in heaven; and make us to know that all things are possible to us through thy Son, our Redeemer Jesus Christ.

B. F. Westcott

The North Presbytery Aisle

On the right-hand side is the Chantry Chapel of the last Abbot of the monastery, William Ramryge, who died in about 1520. There are many rams carved here, and each ram has a collar bearing the letters 'RYGE'. The Abbot wanted to make sure that his name would not be forgotten!

In front of the chapel is a fine fourteenth-century brass of the greatest of all the Abbots, Thomas de la Mare. Although he lived until he was nearly ninety, the brass image has a very young face. Images of revered and holy men were sometimes given the face of a man in his early thirties so as to echo the age at which Jesus died. Or perhaps the youthful face of the image of Thomas was meant to symbolize the belief that in the resurrection all people will be raised in the beauty of youth. Or alternatively, perhaps Thomas commissioned this brass when he was still a young man, because the Black Death was raging at the time and he wanted to be sure that he would be remembered.

The Abbot commissioned this brass and also one of his predecessor, Michael Mentmore, in the early 1350s from a Tournai workshop. Both were origi- nally in front of the High Altar screen. Mentmore's brass probably disappeared during the Cromwellian period; de la Mare's brass survived because it was turned face down to keep it hidden.

Turning back from this point, we can see a seventeenth-century painting of King Offa, the founder of the monastery, high up on the wall. At the end of the aisle on the right is the back of the Watching Chamber. Some lovely carvings can be seen depicting scenes from everyday life in medieval England. Opposite are the remains of the shrine of St Amphibalus, the priest who converted Alban to Christianity.

Prayer

O Lord God, when thou givest to thy servants to endeavour any great matter, grant us also to know that it is not the beginning, but the continuing of the same, until it be thoroughly finished, which yieldeth the true glory; through him who for the finishing of thy work laid down his life for us, our Redeemer, Jesus Christ.

After Sir Francis Drake

The Lady Chapel

This beautiful chapel is dedicated to Our Lady the Blessed Virgin Mary, the mother of Jesus. It was built in the fourteenth century and restored in the nineteenth. When the monastery was dissolved in 1539 this chapel was separated from the rest of the Abbey Church by a wall. There was a public passageway between the chapel and the Shrine. The chapel was used as a school from the Reformation until Victorian times.

The little statues at the sides of the windows were badly damaged during this time. In each window the bottom statue has been almost completely destroyed, the middle one is quite badly damaged, but the one at the top has escaped virtually unscathed. Presumably the schoolboys could not reach so high!

The Lady Chapel is one of the most beautiful parts of the Cathedral, and it is here that most of the weddings and funerals take place. The services of other Christian denominations are also held here. Because St Alban was martyred long before the Church was divided, and since it is only as a result of the accidents of history that the Abbey is looked after today by the Church of England, so we believe that it belongs to all the Christian people in the city.

Thus, to our great delight, since 1983 a Roman Catholic mass has been said every Friday at noon in this Lady Chapel. At the end of the mass the congregation all turn to face the Shrine of St Alban as we pray for Christian unity. There is also a Free Church Service, led by a Baptist, Methodist or United Reformed minister or a Salvation Army Officer, on two Wednesdays in every month. An Orthodox liturgy is celebrated twice a year, and, once a month, there is a service for German-speaking Lutherans living in Hertfordshire. In addition to this there are, of course, big united services in the Nave throughout the year, and we are glad to have four Ecumenical Chaplains (Roman Catholic, Free Church, Orthodox and Lutheran) as honorary members of the Cathedral staff.

The Shrine from the Lady Chapel

Prayer

Behold, how good and joyful a thing it is to dwell together in unity.

Psalm 133:1

*

We thank God for the links which bind us to our fellow Christians throughout the world; for the tasks in which we co-operate; for the truths we hold in common.

We pray for all those who are working for the unity of Christ's Church; for local congregations who are learning from each other; for all our fellow Christians of other traditions.

Now unto him that is able to do exceeding abundantly above all that we ask or think according to the power that worketh in us, to him be glory in the Church by Christ Jesus, throughout all ages, world without end.

Ephesians 3:20–21

✠

During the summer months there is always a priest or minister on duty in the Cathedral as 'chaplain for the day'. These are usually parish priests from the

41

Diocese who come to spend a day here just to be available for anyone who wants to talk. However, clergy from the other Christian churches also play a full part in this work, acting as Chaplains every week. As was mentioned earlier, every hour on the hour the Chaplain asks everyone in the building to be still just for a moment while he or she says a prayer to remind us that this is a House of God, a living place of worship.

Prayers

Nothing in all creation is so like God as stillness.

Meister Eckhart

*

Like as the hart desireth the water-brooks:
so longeth my soul after thee, O God.
My soul is athirst for God,
Yea, even for the living God.

Psalm 42:1

The Shrine of St Alban

The climax of any pilgrim's visit to St Albans has always been to pray at the Shrine. Before the two great screens were built it was possible to stand at the entrance at the far West End and look right up the whole length of the building to see the Shrine standing in glory. Here, for over 1,700 years, pilgrims have come to pray to God. In medieval times they often came to pray for healing. Still today, healing services are held here and prayers are said for the sick. The Holy Eucharist is celebrated at the Shrine Altar.

The Shrine pedestal was made in the early fourteenth century from Purbeck marble. It replaced an earlier 'table' pedestal (as shown in Matthew Paris' chronicles of the Cathedral). Alban's remains would have been on the top of the Shrine pedestal under a canopy. They were kept in a beautiful jewelled reliquary, which was paraded around the Abbey on special occasions such as St Alban's Day.

The Saint's bones are no longer here because in 1539 emissaries from King Henry VIII came to St Albans with the express purpose of destroying the bones, taking the priceless reliquary to boost the King's coffers and smashing the marble pedestal on which the reliquary stood. It lay in pieces for hundreds of years until Victorian restorers carefully pieced together as many fragments as they could find. Further restoration took place in 1993 in honour of the 1,200th anniversary of the founding of the monastery, and a new canopy was fitted.

A monk used to stand at the west end of the Shrine chronicling the miraculous healings that took place. In the medieval Watching Chamber, with its upstairs windows, the monks used to keep guard over the Shrine.

Although Alban's remains are here no longer, many pilgrims still come to kneel at his Shrine. The Alban Prayer is placed along the rails in English, French, German, Italian and Spanish. Many pilgrims also light a candle. While you are here you may wish to thank God for your pilgrimage or to pray for someone you love or someone in need or trouble. Or you may want just to kneel and be quiet.

Our Lord Jesus said: 'Let your light so shine before men that they may see your good works and glorify your Father who is in heaven' (Matthew 5:16). The flames of the candles burn steadily as symbols of hope and as a sign that the light of Christ is alive and shining in a dark world. Wherever Christ is made known, light dawns.

The Shrine

Prayer

Among the roses of the martyrs
Brightly shines St Alban.

✠

Almighty God,
we thank you for this place
built to your glory
and in memory of Alban,
our first martyr:
Following his example
in the fellowship of the Saints,
may we worship and adore
the true and living God,
and be faithful witnesses
to the Christ,
who is alive and reigns,
now and for ever. Amen.

Humphrey, Duke of Gloucester

Opposite the Shrine, on the other side of the Watching Chamber, is an iron grille in the floor. This covers the vault of Humphrey, Duke of Gloucester, the brother of King Henry V and the only royal person buried in the Abbey. Duke Humphrey was the Lord Protector of England for the young King Henry VI. He founded the University Library at Oxford (now known as the Bodleian) and was a great benefactor of the Abbey. He wished to be buried as near as possible to St Alban.

Humphrey appears in Shakespeare's *Henry VI Part I*. In Act 2 there is a scene in which the townspeople of St Albans, led by the Mayor, bring in a beggar named Simcox. This crafty man claims that, although blind from birth and also lame, he has been cured of his blindness that morning by a miracle at the Shrine of St Alban. Humphrey asks him about the colour of various cloaks and Simcox gives the right answers. But how, asks Humphrey, if he has been blind from birth, could he have known all the different colours? He orders the beggar to be beaten, but gives him the chance to run away. Simcox refuses, claiming to be lame, but at the third stroke he leaps over a stool and runs as fast as his legs can carry him. 'Duke Humphrey has done a miracle today,' says the Cardinal.

The statues on the upper section of the tomb (in the archway) are believed to be the only pre-Reformation statues surviving in the Abbey. They can be seen from the south ambulatory aisle. They survived because they are statues of kings, not of religious figures such as saints.

The canopy above St Alban's Shrine

O Lord Jesus Christ, who has made me and
redeemed me
and brought me where I am upon my way:
thou knowest what thou wouldst do with me;
do with me according to thy will,
for thy tender mercies' sake.

King Henry VI

*

Lord, give me patience in tribulation
and grace in everything
to conform my will to thine
that I may truly say:
thy will be done on earth as in heaven.

St Thomas More

The Chapel of the Four Tapers

In this chapel, so named because there used to be four candles round the altar, is the small sculptured figure of a medieval knight called Sir William Clinton. As far as we know, he was not an ancestor of the American President of that name, but we can't resist pointing him out, especially to visitors from America! There are some people who believe that the statue is actually not of Sir William but of St George, with one foot slightly raised as if on a dragon. The statue was discarded as rubbish during Lord Grimthorpe's restoration in the nineteenth century, but it was later rescued and returned to the Abbey.

Today this chapel is used by the Mothers' Union, and here we pray especially for our own families; for those whom we love and those who love us; for those for whom we have care and responsibility, and those who care for us.

Sir William Clinton

The South Presbytery Aisle

In this aisle there is the little Chantry Chapel of Abbot William of Wallingford, the builder of the High Altar screen. This chapel is now kept for private prayer, and here the Blessed Sacrament is reserved.

✠

Prayers

> Be still and know that I am God.
>
> Psalm 46:10

*

We thank God that in the Blessed Sacrament Christ comes to us, in forgiveness and in love, to unite us with himself; that here we have a living reminder of his death and resurrection and of his presence with us always.

*

And then for those, our dearest and our best,
　By this prevailing presence we appeal;
O fold them closer to Thy mercy's breast,
O do Thine utmost for their souls' true weal.

English Hymnal, 302

Just past the chapel there is an old seventeenth-century poor box on the floor, and on the wall above it there is a twentieth-century copy of a carved and painted figure of a man from about 1680. The original is in the Treasury.

The South Transept

High up on the wall of this transept are some Saxon pilasters (small pillars). The staircase, known as the Michael Stair, is in memory of Bishop Michael Gresford Jones, Bishop of St Albans. It dates from the 1980s and is based on the old stone staircase in Hexham Abbey in Northumberland. At its foot is a little alcove where in times past loaves used to be left for twenty-four widows every Saturday morning. At the top is a Latin inscription from the Old Testament: 'Remember me, O my God, concerning this and wipe not out my good deeds that I have done for the house of my God and for his service' (Nehemiah 13:14). The staircase, which is used by clergy and choir, leads to the vestry and the first floor of the Chapter House.

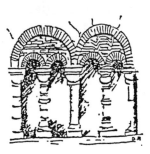

Saxon pilasters

The Chapter House

The present Chapter House, opened by the Queen in 1982, stands on the site of the old monastic chapter house. Refreshments can be obtained in the Refectory. Also on the ground floor are the Information Desk and the Gift Shop. Upstairs there is a library of modern theological books, the clergy vestry and the Cathedral offices. Higher still is the Song School for the Choir. Downstairs is a modern crypt used for youth work and other activities.

The Hudson Memorial Library is named after a twentieth-century canon of the Cathedral, Cyril Hudson. One of his claims to fame (apart from endowing his books to the Cathedral) is that in his younger days, when he was a curate at Berkhamsted, he was the only person to give the schoolboy Michael Hordern any theatrical encouragement. Thanks to him, Sir Michael went on to become a famous actor, playing many different parts, ranging from King Lear to the voice of Paddington Bear!

Outside the Chapter House is Sumpter Yard, where supplies for the monastery used to be unloaded from pack animals, and where supplies for the Refectory are unloaded still. In the Yard stands a huge and impressive cedar tree brought from Lebanon by

Countess Spencer and planted in 1803.

Sumpter Yard is not a cathedral close, but leads right into the city. From it we go back into the world outside. Please remember in your prayers the Cathedral and Abbey Church of St Alban and those who work here. This is a building which lifts up our hearts and points us to God, who is with us always.

Pilgrimage to St Albans

Prayers

May we leave this holy place, the site of the death of Britain's first Christian martyr, with renewed faith and hope. As we remember Alban and all the Saints, may we too worship and adore the true and living God, and be faithful witnesses to the Christ who is alive and reigns now and for ever.

*

Lord, make me see your glory in every place.

Michaelangelo

*

Teach me, my God and King,
In all things thee to see,
And what I do in any way
To do it as for thee.

George Herbert

*

O Lord Jesus Christ,
Take our minds and think through them,
Take our lips and speak through them,
Take our hands and work through them,
Take our hearts and set them on fire
with love for Thee,
now and always. Amen.

*

Remember, O Lord, what Thou hast wrought in us, and not what we deserve; and, as Thou hast called us to Thy service, make us worthy of our calling; through Jesus Christ our Lord.

Leonine Sacramentary

*

The hands of the Father uphold you,
The hands of the Saviour enfold you,
The hands of the Spirit surround you
And the blessing of God Almighty
Father, Son and Holy Spirit
Be upon you and remain with you, always.

Celtic prayer